MINDFULNESS JOURNAL: DAILY CHECK-IN

Mindfulness Journal
DAILY CHECK-IN

PROMPTS TO MOTIVATE, TRACK, AND OBSERVE YOUR MINDFULNESS PRACTICE

Kristen Manieri

ROCKRIDGE
PRESS

For general information on our other products and services or to obtain technical support, please contact our Customer Care Department within the United States at (866) 744-2665, or outside the United States at (510) 253-0500.

Rockridge Press publishes its books in a variety of electronic and print formats. Some content that appears in print may not be available in electronic books, and vice versa.

Interior and Cover Designer: Erik Jacobsen
Art Producer: Janice Ackerman
Production Editor: Andrew Yackira
Production Manager: Riley Hoffman

Author photo courtesy of Arlene Laboy
Illustration: ©NKate/Creative Market

ISBN: Print 978-1-63807-812-8
R0

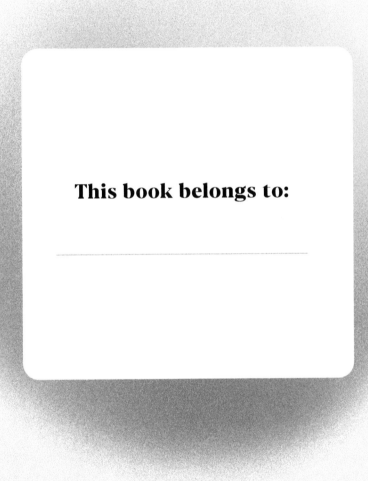

This book belongs to:

_____

Introduction

We are always in process, never complete. Even when we're unaware of it, we continuously grow and evolve. To be actively engaged in this process is a hallmark of being human. We can think about our thinking; we can reflect on the living of our lives. The more we do so, the more we grow.

Mindfulness is our ability to bring a curious and judgment-free awareness to our experiences inside and around us, but it is also what helps us know ourselves more deeply. Each time we bring presence to our individual experience of living, we begin to access not only our awareness but also our inner wisdom.

This journal is designed to support daily engagement with your work in progress: this life project of "you." It invites you to consider what matters and to cultivate gratitude, insight, and authenticity. It creates the space for an inside conversation where you can reflect on your intentions and priorities with curiosity and openness. What you learn can help you mindfully guide your way forward with intention. To actively engage in your growth is to steer your own ship.

As you meet yourself on the following pages over the next 90 days, you'll get to know yourself better, perhaps finding a friend and support system you may not have known was there. You matter. You are worth the time it takes to excavate who you really are and what makes your life feel good. Let's get started!

Morning Intentions

What thoughts and feelings are present for me in this moment?

_____

_____

_____

How can I set myself up to bring my best self to the world today?

_____

_____

What am I joyfully anticipating in the day(s) ahead?

_____

I'd like to create more _____ in my life by:

_____

Ways I intend to feel grounded today:

☐ Three deep breaths

☐ 60-second body scan

☐ Mindful check-in

Date: ___ / ___ / ___

What is one thing today's experiences teach me about myself?

_____

_____

I'm ready to have this question answered:

_____

_____

Use this space to track how you practiced mindfulness throughout the day.

	When	Where
Morning		
Afternoon		
Evening		

Three things I am grateful for:

Morning Intentions

Date: ___ / ___ / ___

What thoughts and feelings are present for me in this moment?

_____

_____

_____

How can I set myself up to bring my best self to the world today?

_____

_____

What am I joyfully anticipating in the day(s) ahead?

_____

I'd like to create more _____ in my life by:

_____

Ways I intend to feel grounded today:

☐ Three deep breaths

☐ 60-second body scan

☐ Mindful check-in

Date: ___ / ___ / ___

What is one thing today's experiences teach me about myself?

_____

_____

I'm ready to have this question answered:

_____

_____

Use this space to track how you practiced mindfulness throughout the day.

	When	Where
Morning		
Afternoon		
Evening		

Three things I am grateful for:

Morning Intentions

What thoughts and feelings are present for me in this moment?

_____

_____

_____

How can I set myself up to bring my best self to the world today?

_____

_____

What am I joyfully anticipating in the day(s) ahead?

_____

I'd like to create more _____ in my life by:

_____

Ways I intend to feel grounded today:

☐ Three deep breaths

☐ 60-second body scan

☐ Mindful check-in

Date: ___ / ___ / ___

What is one thing today's experiences teach me about myself?

_____

_____

I'm ready to have this question answered:

_____

_____

Use this space to track how you practiced mindfulness throughout the day.

	When	Where
Morning		
Afternoon		
Evening		

Three things I am grateful for:

Morning Intentions

What thoughts and feelings are present for me in this moment?

_____

_____

_____

How can I set myself up to bring my best self to the world today?

_____

_____

What am I joyfully anticipating in the day(s) ahead?

_____

I'd like to create more _____ in my life by:

_____

Ways I intend to feel grounded today:

☐ Three deep breaths

☐ 60-second body scan

☐ Mindful check-in

Evening Reflections

What is one thing today's experiences teach me about myself?

_____

_____

I'm ready to have this question answered:

_____

_____

Use this space to track how you practiced mindfulness throughout the day.

	When	Where
Morning		
Afternoon		
Evening		

Three things I am grateful for:

Morning Intentions

What thoughts and feelings are present for me in this moment?

_____

_____

_____

How can I set myself up to bring my best self to the world today?

_____

_____

What am I joyfully anticipating in the day(s) ahead?

_____

I'd like to create more _____ in my life by:

_____

Ways I intend to feel grounded today:

☐ Three deep breaths

☐ 60-second body scan

☐ Mindful check-in

Date: ___ / ___ / ___

What is one thing today's experiences teach me about myself?

_____

_____

I'm ready to have this question answered:

_____

_____

Use this space to track how you practiced mindfulness throughout the day.

	When	Where
Morning		
Afternoon		
Evening		

Three things I am grateful for:

Date: ___ / ___ / ___

What thoughts and feelings are present for me in this moment?

_____

_____

_____

How can I set myself up to bring my best self to the world today?

_____

_____

What am I joyfully anticipating in the day(s) ahead?

_____

I'd like to create more _____ in my life by:

_____

Ways I intend to feel grounded today:

☐ Three deep breaths

☐ 60-second body scan

☐ Mindful check-in

Date: ___ / ___ / ___   Evening Reflections

What is one thing today's experiences teach me about myself?

_____

_____

I'm ready to have this question answered:

_____

_____

Use this space to track how you practiced mindfulness throughout the day.

	When	Where
Morning		
Afternoon		
Evening		

Three things I am grateful for:

What thoughts and feelings are present for me in this moment?

_____

_____

_____

How can I set myself up to bring my best self to the world today?

_____

_____

What am I joyfully anticipating in the day(s) ahead?

_____

I'd like to create more _____ in my life by:

_____

Ways I intend to feel grounded today:

☐ Three deep breaths

☐ 60-second body scan

☐ Mindful check-in

Date: ___ / ___ / ___

What is one thing today's experiences teach me about myself?

_____

_____

I'm ready to have this question answered:

_____

_____

Use this space to track how you practiced mindfulness throughout the day.

	When	Where
Morning		
Afternoon		
Evening		

Three things I am grateful for:

Morning Intentions

What thoughts and feelings are present for me in this moment?

_____

_____

_____

How can I set myself up to bring my best self to the world today?

_____

_____

What am I joyfully anticipating in the day(s) ahead?

_____

I'd like to create more _____ in my life by:

_____

Ways I intend to feel grounded today:

☐ Three deep breaths

☐ 60-second body scan

☐ Mindful check-in

Date: ___ / ___ / ___

What is one thing today's experiences teach me about myself?

_____

_____

I'm ready to have this question answered:

_____

_____

Use this space to track how you practiced mindfulness throughout the day.

	When	Where
Morning		
Afternoon		
Evening		

Three things I am grateful for:

What thoughts and feelings are present for me in this moment?

_____

_____

_____

How can I set myself up to bring my best self to the world today?

_____

_____

What am I joyfully anticipating in the day(s) ahead?

_____

I'd like to create more _____ in my life by:

_____

Ways I intend to feel grounded today:

☐ Three deep breaths

☐ 60-second body scan

☐ Mindful check-in

Date: ___ / ___ / ___   ## Evening Reflections

What is one thing today's experiences teach me about myself?

_____

_____

I'm ready to have this question answered:

_____

_____

Use this space to track how you practiced mindfulness throughout the day.

	When	Where
Morning		
Afternoon		
Evening		

Three things I am grateful for:

Morning Intentions

What thoughts and feelings are present for me in this moment?

_____

_____

_____

How can I set myself up to bring my best self to the world today?

_____

_____

What am I joyfully anticipating in the day(s) ahead?

_____

I'd like to create more _____ in my life by:

_____

Ways I intend to feel grounded today:

☐ Three deep breaths

☐ 60-second body scan

☐ Mindful check-in

Date: ___ / ___ / ___

What is one thing today's experiences teach me about myself?

_____

_____

I'm ready to have this question answered:

_____

_____

Use this space to track how you practiced mindfulness throughout the day.

	When	Where
Morning		
Afternoon		
Evening		

Three things I am grateful for:

Morning Intentions

What thoughts and feelings are present for me in this moment?

_____

_____

_____

How can I set myself up to bring my best self to the world today?

_____

_____

What am I joyfully anticipating in the day(s) ahead?

_____

I'd like to create more _____ in my life by:

_____

Ways I intend to feel grounded today:

☐ Three deep breaths

☐ 60-second body scan

☐ Mindful check-in

Date: ___ / ___ / ___

What is one thing today's experiences teach me about myself?

_____

_____

I'm ready to have this question answered:

_____

_____

Use this space to track how you practiced mindfulness throughout the day.

	When	Where
Morning		
Afternoon		
Evening		

Three things I am grateful for:

Date: ___ / ___ / ___

What thoughts and feelings are present for me in this moment?

_____

_____

_____

How can I set myself up to bring my best self to the world today?

_____

_____

What am I joyfully anticipating in the day(s) ahead?

_____

I'd like to create more _____ in my life by:

_____

Ways I intend to feel grounded today:

☐ Three deep breaths

☐ 60-second body scan

☐ Mindful check-in

Date: ___ / ___ / ___   **Evening Reflections**

What is one thing today's experiences teach me about myself?

_____

_____

I'm ready to have this question answered:

_____

_____

Use this space to track how you practiced mindfulness throughout the day.

	When	Where
Morning		
Afternoon		
Evening		

Three things I am grateful for:

Morning Intentions

What thoughts and feelings are present for me in this moment?

_____

_____

_____

How can I set myself up to bring my best self to the world today?

_____

_____

What am I joyfully anticipating in the day(s) ahead?

_____

I'd like to create more _____ in my life by:

_____

Ways I intend to feel grounded today:

☐ Three deep breaths

☐ 60-second body scan

☐ Mindful check-in

Date: ___ / ___ / ___

What is one thing today's experiences teach me about myself?

_____

_____

I'm ready to have this question answered:

_____

_____

Use this space to track how you practiced mindfulness throughout the day.

	When	Where
Morning		
Afternoon		
Evening		

Three things I am grateful for:

Morning Intentions

What thoughts and feelings are present for me in this moment?

_____

_____

_____

How can I set myself up to bring my best self to the
world today?

_____

_____

What am I joyfully anticipating in the day(s) ahead?

_____

I'd like to create more _____ in my life by:

_____

Ways I intend to feel grounded today:

☐ Three deep breaths

☐ 60-second body scan

☐ Mindful check-in

Date: ___/___/___

Evening Reflections

What is one thing today's experiences teach me about myself?

I'm ready to have this question answered:

Use this space to track how you practiced mindfulness throughout the day.

	When	Where
Morning		
Afternoon		
Evening		

Three things I am grateful for:

Morning Intentions

What thoughts and feelings are present for me in this moment?

_____

_____

_____

How can I set myself up to bring my best self to the world today?

_____

_____

What am I joyfully anticipating in the day(s) ahead?

_____

I'd like to create more _____ in my life by:

_____

Ways I intend to feel grounded today:

☐ Three deep breaths

☐ 60-second body scan

☐ Mindful check-in

Date: ___ / ___ / ___   Evening Reflections

What is one thing today's experiences teach me about myself?

_____

_____

I'm ready to have this question answered:

_____

_____

Use this space to track how you practiced mindfulness throughout the day.

	When	Where
Morning		
Afternoon		
Evening		

Three things I am grateful for:

Date: ___ / ___ / ___

What thoughts and feelings are present for me in this moment?

_____

_____

_____

How can I set myself up to bring my best self to the world today?

_____

_____

What am I joyfully anticipating in the day(s) ahead?

_____

I'd like to create more _____ in my life by:

_____

Ways I intend to feel grounded today:

☐ Three deep breaths

☐ 60-second body scan

☐ Mindful check-in

Date: ___ / ___ / ___

What is one thing today's experiences teach me about myself?

_____

_____

I'm ready to have this question answered:

_____

_____

Use this space to track how you practiced mindfulness throughout the day.

	When	Where
Morning		
Afternoon		
Evening		

Three things I am grateful for:

Morning Intentions

What thoughts and feelings are present for me in this moment?

_____

_____

_____

How can I set myself up to bring my best self to the
world today?

_____

_____

What am I joyfully anticipating in the day(s) ahead?

_____

I'd like to create more _____ in my life by:

_____

Ways I intend to feel grounded today:

☐ Three deep breaths

☐ 60-second body scan

☐ Mindful check-in

Date: ___ / ___ / ___

What is one thing today's experiences teach me about myself?

_____

_____

I'm ready to have this question answered:

_____

_____

Use this space to track how you practiced mindfulness throughout the day.

	When	Where
Morning		
Afternoon		
Evening		

Three things I am grateful for:

Morning Intentions

What thoughts and feelings are present for me in this moment?

_____

_____

_____

How can I set myself up to bring my best self to the world today?

_____

_____

What am I joyfully anticipating in the day(s) ahead?

_____

I'd like to create more _____ in my life by:

_____

Ways I intend to feel grounded today:

☐ Three deep breaths

☐ 60-second body scan

☐ Mindful check-in

Evening Reflections

What is one thing today's experiences teach me about myself?

_____

_____

I'm ready to have this question answered:

_____

_____

Use this space to track how you practiced mindfulness throughout the day.

	When	Where
Morning		
Afternoon		
Evening		

Three things I am grateful for:

Morning Intentions

What thoughts and feelings are present for me in this moment?

_____

_____

_____

How can I set myself up to bring my best self to the world today?

_____

_____

What am I joyfully anticipating in the day(s) ahead?

_____

I'd like to create more _____ in my life by:

_____

Ways I intend to feel grounded today:

☐ Three deep breaths

☐ 60-second body scan

☐ Mindful check-in

Date: ___ / ___ / ___

What is one thing today's experiences teach me about myself?

_____

_____

I'm ready to have this question answered:

_____

_____

Use this space to track how you practiced mindfulness throughout the day.

	When	Where
Morning		
Afternoon		
Evening		

Three things I am grateful for:

What thoughts and feelings are present for me in this moment?

_____

_____

_____

How can I set myself up to bring my best self to the world today?

_____

_____

What am I joyfully anticipating in the day(s) ahead?

_____

I'd like to create more _____ in my life by:

_____

Ways I intend to feel grounded today:

☐ Three deep breaths

☐ 60-second body scan

☐ Mindful check-in

Date: ___ / ___ / ___

What is one thing today's experiences teach me about myself?

_____

_____

I'm ready to have this question answered:

_____

_____

Use this space to track how you practiced mindfulness throughout the day.

	When	Where
Morning		
Afternoon		
Evening		

Three things I am grateful for:

Morning Intentions

Date: ___ / ___ / ___

What thoughts and feelings are present for me in this moment?

_____

_____

_____

How can I set myself up to bring my best self to the world today?

_____

_____

What am I joyfully anticipating in the day(s) ahead?

_____

I'd like to create more _____ in my life by:

_____

Ways I intend to feel grounded today:

☐ Three deep breaths

☐ 60-second body scan

☐ Mindful check-in

Date: ___ / ___ / ___

Evening Reflections

What is one thing today's experiences teach me about myself?

_____

_____

I'm ready to have this question answered:

_____

_____

Use this space to track how you practiced mindfulness throughout the day.

	When	Where
Morning		
Afternoon		
Evening		

Three things I am grateful for:

Morning Intentions

What thoughts and feelings are present for me in this moment?

_____

_____

_____

How can I set myself up to bring my best self to the world today?

_____

_____

What am I joyfully anticipating in the day(s) ahead?

_____

I'd like to create more _____ in my life by:

_____

Ways I intend to feel grounded today:

☐ Three deep breaths

☐ 60-second body scan

☐ Mindful check-in

Evening Reflections

What is one thing today's experiences teach me about myself?

_____

_____

I'm ready to have this question answered:

_____

_____

Use this space to track how you practiced mindfulness throughout the day.

	When	Where
Morning		
Afternoon		
Evening		

Three things I am grateful for:

Morning Intentions

What thoughts and feelings are present for me in this moment?

_____

_____

_____

How can I set myself up to bring my best self to the world today?

_____

_____

What am I joyfully anticipating in the day(s) ahead?

_____

I'd like to create more _____ in my life by:

_____

Ways I intend to feel grounded today:

☐ Three deep breaths

☐ 60-second body scan

☐ Mindful check-in

Date: ___ / ___ / ___

What is one thing today's experiences teach me about myself?

_____

_____

I'm ready to have this question answered:

_____

_____

Use this space to track how you practiced mindfulness throughout the day.

	When	Where
Morning		
Afternoon		
Evening		

Three things I am grateful for:

What thoughts and feelings are present for me in this moment?

_____

_____

_____

How can I set myself up to bring my best self to the world today?

_____

_____

What am I joyfully anticipating in the day(s) ahead?

_____

I'd like to create more _____ in my life by:

_____

Ways I intend to feel grounded today:

☐ Three deep breaths

☐ 60-second body scan

☐ Mindful check-in

Date: __ / __ / __   Evening Reflections

What is one thing today's experiences teach me about myself?

_____

_____

I'm ready to have this question answered:

_____

_____

Use this space to track how you practiced mindfulness throughout the day.

	When	Where
Morning		
Afternoon		
Evening		

Three things I am grateful for:

Morning Intentions

What thoughts and feelings are present for me in this moment?

_____

_____

_____

How can I set myself up to bring my best self to the world today?

_____

_____

What am I joyfully anticipating in the day(s) ahead?

_____

I'd like to create more _____ in my life by:

_____

Ways I intend to feel grounded today:

☐ Three deep breaths

☐ 60-second body scan

☐ Mindful check-in

Date: ___ / ___ / ___   Evening Reflections

What is one thing today's experiences teach me about myself?

_____

_____

I'm ready to have this question answered:

_____

_____

Use this space to track how you practiced mindfulness throughout the day.

	When	Where
Morning		
Afternoon		
Evening		

Three things I am grateful for:

Morning Intentions

What thoughts and feelings are present for me in this moment?

_____

_____

_____

How can I set myself up to bring my best self to the world today?

_____

_____

What am I joyfully anticipating in the day(s) ahead?

_____

I'd like to create more _____ in my life by:

_____

Ways I intend to feel grounded today:

☐ Three deep breaths

☐ 60-second body scan

☐ Mindful check-in

Date: ___ / ___ / ___

What is one thing today's experiences teach me about myself?

_____

_____

I'm ready to have this question answered:

_____

_____

Use this space to track how you practiced mindfulness throughout the day.

	When	Where
Morning		
Afternoon		
Evening		

Three things I am grateful for:

Date: ___ / ___ / ___

What thoughts and feelings are present for me in this moment?

_____

_____

_____

How can I set myself up to bring my best self to the world today?

_____

_____

What am I joyfully anticipating in the day(s) ahead?

_____

I'd like to create more _____ in my life by:

_____

Ways I intend to feel grounded today:

☐ Three deep breaths

☐ 60-second body scan

☐ Mindful check-in

Evening Reflections

What is one thing today's experiences teach me about myself?

_____

_____

I'm ready to have this question answered:

_____

_____

Use this space to track how you practiced mindfulness throughout the day.

	When	Where
Morning		
Afternoon		
Evening		

Three things I am grateful for:

Morning Intentions

What thoughts and feelings are present for me in this moment?

_____

_____

_____

How can I set myself up to bring my best self to the world today?

_____

_____

What am I joyfully anticipating in the day(s) ahead?

_____

I'd like to create more _____ in my life by:

_____

Ways I intend to feel grounded today:

☐ Three deep breaths

☐ 60-second body scan

☐ Mindful check-in

Evening Reflections

What is one thing today's experiences teach me about myself?

_____

_____

I'm ready to have this question answered:

_____

_____

Use this space to track how you practiced mindfulness throughout the day.

	When	Where
Morning		
Afternoon		
Evening		

Three things I am grateful for:

Morning Intentions

What thoughts and feelings are present for me in this moment?

_____

_____

_____

How can I set myself up to bring my best self to the world today?

_____

_____

What am I joyfully anticipating in the day(s) ahead?

_____

I'd like to create more _____ in my life by:

_____

Ways I intend to feel grounded today:

☐ Three deep breaths

☐ 60-second body scan

☐ Mindful check-in

Date: ___ / ___ / ___

What is one thing today's experiences teach me about myself?

_____

_____

I'm ready to have this question answered:

_____

_____

Use this space to track how you practiced mindfulness throughout the day.

	When	Where
Morning		
Afternoon		
Evening		

Three things I am grateful for:

Morning Intentions

What thoughts and feelings are present for me in this moment?

_____

_____

_____

How can I set myself up to bring my best self to the world today?

_____

_____

What am I joyfully anticipating in the day(s) ahead?

_____

I'd like to create more _____ in my life by:

_____

Ways I intend to feel grounded today:

☐ Three deep breaths

☐ 60-second body scan

☐ Mindful check-in

Date: ___ / ___ / ___

What is one thing today's experiences teach me about myself?

_____

_____

I'm ready to have this question answered:

_____

_____

Use this space to track how you practiced mindfulness throughout the day.

	When	Where
Morning		
Afternoon		
Evening		

Three things I am grateful for:

Morning Intentions

What thoughts and feelings are present for me in this moment?

_____

_____

_____

How can I set myself up to bring my best self to the world today?

_____

_____

What am I joyfully anticipating in the day(s) ahead?

_____

I'd like to create more _____ in my life by:

_____

Ways I intend to feel grounded today:

☐ Three deep breaths

☐ 60-second body scan

☐ Mindful check-in

Date: ___ / ___ / ___

What is one thing today's experiences teach me about myself?

_____

_____

I'm ready to have this question answered:

_____

_____

Use this space to track how you practiced mindfulness throughout the day.

	When	Where
Morning		
Afternoon		
Evening		

Three things I am grateful for:

Morning Intentions

What thoughts and feelings are present for me in this moment?

_____

_____

_____

How can I set myself up to bring my best self to the world today?

_____

_____

What am I joyfully anticipating in the day(s) ahead?

_____

I'd like to create more _____ in my life by:

_____

Ways I intend to feel grounded today:

☐ Three deep breaths

☐ 60-second body scan

☐ Mindful check-in

Date: ___ / ___ / ___   **Evening Reflections**

What is one thing today's experiences teach me about myself?

_____

_____

I'm ready to have this question answered:

_____

_____

Use this space to track how you practiced mindfulness throughout the day.

	When	Where
Morning		
Afternoon		
Evening		

Three things I am grateful for:

What thoughts and feelings are present for me in this moment?

_____

_____

_____

How can I set myself up to bring my best self to the world today?

_____

_____

What am I joyfully anticipating in the day(s) ahead?

_____

I'd like to create more _____ in my life by:

_____

Ways I intend to feel grounded today:

☐ Three deep breaths

☐ 60-second body scan

☐ Mindful check-in

Date: ___ / ___ / ___   **Evening Reflections**

What is one thing today's experiences teach me about myself?

_____

_____

I'm ready to have this question answered:

_____

_____

Use this space to track how you practiced mindfulness throughout the day.

	When	Where
Morning		
Afternoon		
Evening		

Three things I am grateful for:

Morning Intentions

What thoughts and feelings are present for me in this moment?

_____

_____

_____

How can I set myself up to bring my best self to the world today?

_____

_____

What am I joyfully anticipating in the day(s) ahead?

_____

I'd like to create more _____ in my life by:

_____

Ways I intend to feel grounded today:

☐ Three deep breaths

☐ 60-second body scan

☐ Mindful check-in

Date: ___ / ___ / ___   Evening Reflections

What is one thing today's experiences teach me about myself?

_____

_____

I'm ready to have this question answered:

_____

_____

Use this space to track how you practiced mindfulness throughout the day.

	When	Where
Morning		
Afternoon		
Evening		

Three things I am grateful for:

Morning Intentions

What thoughts and feelings are present for me in this moment?

_____

_____

_____

How can I set myself up to bring my best self to the world today?

_____

_____

What am I joyfully anticipating in the day(s) ahead?

_____

I'd like to create more _____ in my life by:

_____

Ways I intend to feel grounded today:

☐   Three deep breaths

☐   60-second body scan

☐   Mindful check-in

Date: ___ / ___ / ___

What is one thing today's experiences teach me about myself?

_____

_____

I'm ready to have this question answered:

_____

_____

Use this space to track how you practiced mindfulness throughout the day.

	When	Where
Morning		
Afternoon		
Evening		

Three things I am grateful for:

Morning Intentions

What thoughts and feelings are present for me in this moment?

_____

_____

_____

How can I set myself up to bring my best self to the world today?

_____

_____

What am I joyfully anticipating in the day(s) ahead?

_____

I'd like to create more _____ in my life by:

_____

Ways I intend to feel grounded today:

☐ Three deep breaths

☐ 60-second body scan

☐ Mindful check-in

Date: ___ / ___ / ___   Evening Reflections

What is one thing today's experiences teach me about myself?

_____

_____

I'm ready to have this question answered:

_____

_____

Use this space to track how you practiced mindfulness throughout the day.

	When	Where
Morning		
Afternoon		
Evening		

Three things I am grateful for:

Morning Intentions

What thoughts and feelings are present for me in this moment?

_____

_____

_____

How can I set myself up to bring my best self to the world today?

_____

_____

What am I joyfully anticipating in the day(s) ahead?

_____

I'd like to create more _____ in my life by:

_____

Ways I intend to feel grounded today:

☐ Three deep breaths

☐ 60-second body scan

☐ Mindful check-in

Date: ___ / ___ / ___

What is one thing today's experiences teach me about myself?

_____

_____

I'm ready to have this question answered:

_____

_____

Use this space to track how you practiced mindfulness throughout the day.

	When	Where
Morning		
Afternoon		
Evening		

Three things I am grateful for:

Morning Intentions

What thoughts and feelings are present for me in this moment?

_____

_____

_____

How can I set myself up to bring my best self to the world today?

_____

_____

What am I joyfully anticipating in the day(s) ahead?

_____

I'd like to create more _____ in my life by:

_____

Ways I intend to feel grounded today:

☐ Three deep breaths

☐ 60-second body scan

☐ Mindful check-in

Date: ___ / ___ / ___   # Evening Reflections

What is one thing today's experiences teach me about myself?

_____

_____

I'm ready to have this question answered:

_____

_____

Use this space to track how you practiced mindfulness throughout the day.

	When	Where
Morning		
Afternoon		
Evening		

Three things I am grateful for:

Morning Intentions

What thoughts and feelings are present for me in this moment?

_____

_____

_____

How can I set myself up to bring my best self to the world today?

_____

_____

What am I joyfully anticipating in the day(s) ahead?

_____

I'd like to create more _____ in my life by:

_____

Ways I intend to feel grounded today:

- ☐ Three deep breaths

- ☐ 60-second body scan

- ☐ Mindful check-in

Date: ___ / ___ / ___

Evening Reflections

What is one thing today's experiences teach me about myself?

_____

_____

I'm ready to have this question answered: _____

_____

_____

Use this space to track how you practiced mindfulness throughout the day.

	When	Where
Morning		
Afternoon		
Evening		

Three things I am grateful for:

Morning Intentions

What thoughts and feelings are present for me in this moment?

_____

_____

_____

How can I set myself up to bring my best self to the world today?

_____

_____

What am I joyfully anticipating in the day(s) ahead?

_____

I'd like to create more _____ in my life by:

_____

Ways I intend to feel grounded today:

☐ Three deep breaths

☐ 60-second body scan

☐ Mindful check-in

Date: ___ / ___ / ___

What is one thing today's experiences teach me about myself?

_____

_____

I'm ready to have this question answered:

_____

_____

Use this space to track how you practiced mindfulness throughout the day.

	When	Where
Morning		
Afternoon		
Evening		

Three things I am grateful for:

Morning Intentions

What thoughts and feelings are present for me in this moment?

_____

_____

_____

How can I set myself up to bring my best self to the world today?

_____

_____

What am I joyfully anticipating in the day(s) ahead?

_____

I'd like to create more _____ in my life by:

_____

Ways I intend to feel grounded today:

☐ Three deep breaths

☐ 60-second body scan

☐ Mindful check-in

Date: ___ / ___ / ___

Evening Reflections

What is one thing today's experiences teach me about myself?

_____

_____

I'm ready to have this question answered:

_____

_____

Use this space to track how you practiced mindfulness throughout the day.

	When	Where
Morning		
Afternoon		
Evening		

Three things I am grateful for:

Morning Intentions

What thoughts and feelings are present for me in this moment?

_____

_____

_____

How can I set myself up to bring my best self to the world today?

_____

_____

What am I joyfully anticipating in the day(s) ahead?

_____

I'd like to create more _____ in my life by:

_____

Ways I intend to feel grounded today:

☐ Three deep breaths

☐ 60-second body scan

☐ Mindful check-in

Date: ___ / ___ / ___   ## Evening Reflections

What is one thing today's experiences teach me about myself?

_____

_____

I'm ready to have this question answered:

_____

_____

Use this space to track how you practiced mindfulness throughout the day.

	When	Where
Morning		
Afternoon		
Evening		

Three things I am grateful for:

Morning Intentions

Date: ___ / ___ / ___

What thoughts and feelings are present for me in this moment?

_____

_____

_____

How can I set myself up to bring my best self to the world today?

_____

_____

What am I joyfully anticipating in the day(s) ahead?

_____

I'd like to create more _____ in my life by:

_____

Ways I intend to feel grounded today:

☐ Three deep breaths

☐ 60-second body scan

☐ Mindful check-in

Date: ___ / ___ / ___

Evening Reflections

What is one thing today's experiences teach me about myself?

_____

_____

I'm ready to have this question answered:

_____

_____

Use this space to track how you practiced mindfulness throughout the day.

	When	Where
Morning		
Afternoon		
Evening		

Three things I am grateful for:

Morning Intentions

What thoughts and feelings are present for me in this moment?

_____

_____

_____

How can I set myself up to bring my best self to the world today?

_____

_____

What am I joyfully anticipating in the day(s) ahead?

_____

I'd like to create more _____ in my life by:

_____

Ways I intend to feel grounded today:

☐ Three deep breaths

☐ 60-second body scan

☐ Mindful check-in

Date: ___ / ___ / ___

Evening Reflections

What is one thing today's experiences teach me about myself?

_____

_____

I'm ready to have this question answered:

_____

_____

Use this space to track how you practiced mindfulness throughout the day.

	When	Where
Morning		
Afternoon		
Evening		

Three things I am grateful for:

Morning Intentions

What thoughts and feelings are present for me in this moment?

_____

_____

_____

How can I set myself up to bring my best self to the world today?

_____

_____

What am I joyfully anticipating in the day(s) ahead?

_____

I'd like to create more _____ in my life by:

_____

Ways I intend to feel grounded today:

☐ Three deep breaths

☐ 60-second body scan

☐ Mindful check-in

Date: ___ / ___ / ___

What is one thing today's experiences teach me about myself?

_____

_____

I'm ready to have this question answered:

_____

_____

Use this space to track how you practiced mindfulness throughout the day.

	When	Where
Morning		
Afternoon		
Evening		

Three things I am grateful for:

Morning Intentions

What thoughts and feelings are present for me in this moment?

_____

_____

_____

How can I set myself up to bring my best self to the world today?

_____

_____

What am I joyfully anticipating in the day(s) ahead?

_____

I'd like to create more _____ in my life by:

_____

Ways I intend to feel grounded today:

☐ Three deep breaths

☐ 60-second body scan

☐ Mindful check-in

Date: ___ / ___ / ___

Evening Reflections

What is one thing today's experiences teach me about myself?

_____

_____

I'm ready to have this question answered:

_____

_____

Use this space to track how you practiced mindfulness throughout the day.

	When	Where
Morning		
Afternoon		
Evening		

Three things I am grateful for:

Morning Intentions

What thoughts and feelings are present for me in this moment?

_____

_____

_____

How can I set myself up to bring my best self to the world today?

_____

_____

What am I joyfully anticipating in the day(s) ahead?

_____

I'd like to create more _____ in my life by:

_____

Ways I intend to feel grounded today:

☐ Three deep breaths

☐ 60-second body scan

☐ Mindful check-in

Date: ___ / ___ / ___

Evening Reflections

What is one thing today's experiences teach me about myself?

_____

_____

I'm ready to have this question answered:

_____

_____

Use this space to track how you practiced mindfulness throughout the day.

	When	Where
Morning		
Afternoon		
Evening		

Three things I am grateful for:

Morning Intentions

What thoughts and feelings are present for me in this moment?

_____

_____

_____

How can I set myself up to bring my best self to the world today?

_____

_____

What am I joyfully anticipating in the day(s) ahead?

_____

I'd like to create more _____ in my life by:

_____

Ways I intend to feel grounded today:

☐ Three deep breaths

☐ 60-second body scan

☐ Mindful check-in

Date: ___ / ___ / ___   ## Evening Reflections

What is one thing today's experiences teach me about myself?

_____

_____

I'm ready to have this question answered:

_____

_____

Use this space to track how you practiced mindfulness throughout the day.

	When	Where
Morning		
Afternoon		
Evening		

Three things I am grateful for:

Morning Intentions

What thoughts and feelings are present for me in this moment?

_____

_____

_____

How can I set myself up to bring my best self to the world today?

_____

_____

What am I joyfully anticipating in the day(s) ahead?

_____

I'd like to create more _____ in my life by:

_____

Ways I intend to feel grounded today:

☐ Three deep breaths

☐ 60-second body scan

☐ Mindful check-in

Evening Reflections

What is one thing today's experiences teach me about myself?

_____

_____

I'm ready to have this question answered:

_____

_____

Use this space to track how you practiced mindfulness throughout the day.

	When	Where
Morning		
Afternoon		
Evening		

Three things I am grateful for:

Morning Intentions

What thoughts and feelings are present for me in this moment?

_____

_____

_____

How can I set myself up to bring my best self to the world today?

_____

_____

What am I joyfully anticipating in the day(s) ahead?

_____

I'd like to create more _____ in my life by:

_____

Ways I intend to feel grounded today:

☐ Three deep breaths

☐ 60-second body scan

☐ Mindful check-in

Date: ___ / ___ / ___

Evening Reflections

What is one thing today's experiences teach me about myself?

_____

_____

I'm ready to have this question answered:

_____

_____

Use this space to track how you practiced mindfulness throughout the day.

	When	Where
Morning		
Afternoon		
Evening		

Three things I am grateful for:

Morning Intentions

What thoughts and feelings are present for me in this moment?

_____

_____

_____

How can I set myself up to bring my best self to the world today?

_____

_____

What am I joyfully anticipating in the day(s) ahead?

_____

I'd like to create more _____ in my life by:

_____

Ways I intend to feel grounded today:

☐ Three deep breaths

☐ 60-second body scan

☐ Mindful check-in

Date: ___ / ___ / ___   Evening Reflections

What is one thing today's experiences teach me about myself?

_____

_____

I'm ready to have this question answered:

_____

_____

Use this space to track how you practiced mindfulness throughout the day.

	When	Where
Morning		
Afternoon		
Evening		

Three things I am grateful for:

Morning Intentions

What thoughts and feelings are present for me in this moment?

_____

_____

_____

How can I set myself up to bring my best self to the world today?

_____

_____

What am I joyfully anticipating in the day(s) ahead?

_____

I'd like to create more _____ in my life by:

_____

Ways I intend to feel grounded today:

☐ Three deep breaths

☐ 60-second body scan

☐ Mindful check-in

Date: ___ / ___ / ___   **Evening Reflections**

What is one thing today's experiences teach me about myself?

_____

_____

I'm ready to have this question answered:

_____

_____

Use this space to track how you practiced mindfulness throughout the day.

	When	Where
Morning		
Afternoon		
Evening		

Three things I am grateful for:

Morning Intentions

What thoughts and feelings are present for me in this moment?

_____

_____

_____

How can I set myself up to bring my best self to the world today?

_____

_____

What am I joyfully anticipating in the day(s) ahead?

_____

I'd like to create more _____ in my life by:

_____

Ways I intend to feel grounded today:

☐   Three deep breaths

☐   60-second body scan

☐   Mindful check-in

Date: ___ / ___ / ___

What is one thing today's experiences teach me about myself?

_____

_____

I'm ready to have this question answered:

_____

_____

Use this space to track how you practiced mindfulness throughout the day.

	When	Where
Morning		
Afternoon		
Evening		

Three things I am grateful for:

Morning Intentions

What thoughts and feelings are present for me in this moment?

_____

_____

_____

How can I set myself up to bring my best self to the world today?

_____

_____

What am I joyfully anticipating in the day(s) ahead?

_____

I'd like to create more _____ in my life by:

_____

Ways I intend to feel grounded today:

☐ Three deep breaths

☐ 60-second body scan

☐ Mindful check-in

Date: ___ / ___ / ___

Evening Reflections

What is one thing today's experiences teach me about myself?

_____

_____

I'm ready to have this question answered:

_____

_____

Use this space to track how you practiced mindfulness throughout the day.

	When	Where
Morning		
Afternoon		
Evening		

Three things I am grateful for:

Morning Intentions

What thoughts and feelings are present for me in this moment?

_____

_____

_____

How can I set myself up to bring my best self to the world today?

_____

_____

What am I joyfully anticipating in the day(s) ahead?

_____

I'd like to create more _____ in my life by:

_____

Ways I intend to feel grounded today:

☐ Three deep breaths

☐ 60-second body scan

☐ Mindful check-in

Date: ___ / ___ / ___

What is one thing today's experiences teach me about myself?

_____

_____

I'm ready to have this question answered:

_____

_____

Use this space to track how you practiced mindfulness throughout the day.

	When	Where
Morning		
Afternoon		
Evening		

Three things I am grateful for:

Morning Intentions

What thoughts and feelings are present for me in this moment?

_____

_____

_____

How can I set myself up to bring my best self to the world today?

_____

_____

What am I joyfully anticipating in the day(s) ahead?

_____

I'd like to create more _____ in my life by:

_____

Ways I intend to feel grounded today:

☐ Three deep breaths

☐ 60-second body scan

☐ Mindful check-in

Date: ___ / ___ / ___

What is one thing today's experiences teach me about myself?

_____

_____

I'm ready to have this question answered:

_____

_____

Use this space to track how you practiced mindfulness throughout the day.

	When	Where
Morning		
Afternoon		
Evening		

Three things I am grateful for:

Morning Intentions

What thoughts and feelings are present for me in this moment?

_____

_____

_____

How can I set myself up to bring my best self to the world today?

_____

_____

What am I joyfully anticipating in the day(s) ahead?

_____

I'd like to create more _____ in my life by:

_____

Ways I intend to feel grounded today:

- ☐ Three deep breaths
- ☐ 60-second body scan
- ☐ Mindful check-in

Date: ___ / ___ / ___

What is one thing today's experiences teach me about myself?

_____

_____

I'm ready to have this question answered:

_____

_____

Use this space to track how you practiced mindfulness throughout the day.

	When	Where
Morning		
Afternoon		
Evening		

Three things I am grateful for:

Date: ___ / ___ / ___

What thoughts and feelings are present for me in this moment?

_____

_____

_____

How can I set myself up to bring my best self to the world today?

_____

_____

What am I joyfully anticipating in the day(s) ahead?

_____

I'd like to create more _____ in my life by:

_____

Ways I intend to feel grounded today:

☐ Three deep breaths

☐ 60-second body scan

☐ Mindful check-in

Date: ___ / ___ / ___

What is one thing today's experiences teach me about myself?

_____

_____

I'm ready to have this question answered:

_____

_____

Use this space to track how you practiced mindfulness throughout the day.

	When	Where
Morning		
Afternoon		
Evening		

Three things I am grateful for:

Morning Intentions

Date: ___ / ___ / ___

What thoughts and feelings are present for me in this moment?

_____

_____

_____

How can I set myself up to bring my best self to the world today?

_____

_____

What am I joyfully anticipating in the day(s) ahead?

_____

I'd like to create more _____ in my life by:

_____

Ways I intend to feel grounded today:

☐ Three deep breaths

☐ 60-second body scan

☐ Mindful check-in

Date: ___ / ___ / ___   # Evening Reflections

What is one thing today's experiences teach me about myself?

_____

_____

I'm ready to have this question answered:

_____

_____

Use this space to track how you practiced mindfulness throughout the day.

	When	Where
Morning		
Afternoon		
Evening		

Three things I am grateful for:

Morning Intentions

What thoughts and feelings are present for me in this moment?

_____

_____

_____

How can I set myself up to bring my best self to the world today?

_____

_____

What am I joyfully anticipating in the day(s) ahead?

_____

I'd like to create more _____ in my life by:

_____

Ways I intend to feel grounded today:

☐ Three deep breaths

☐ 60-second body scan

☐ Mindful check-in

Date: ___ / ___ / ___   Evening Reflections

What is one thing today's experiences teach me about myself?

_____

_____

I'm ready to have this question answered:

_____

_____

Use this space to track how you practiced mindfulness throughout the day.

	When	Where
Morning		
Afternoon		
Evening		

Three things I am grateful for:

Morning Intentions

What thoughts and feelings are present for me in this moment?

_____

_____

_____

How can I set myself up to bring my best self to the world today?

_____

_____

What am I joyfully anticipating in the day(s) ahead?

_____

I'd like to create more _____ in my life by:

_____

Ways I intend to feel grounded today:

☐ Three deep breaths

☐ 60-second body scan

☐ Mindful check-in

Date: ___ / ___ / ___

What is one thing today's experiences teach me about myself?

_____

_____

I'm ready to have this question answered:

_____

_____

Use this space to track how you practiced mindfulness throughout the day.

	When	Where
Morning		
Afternoon		
Evening		

Three things I am grateful for:

Morning Intentions

What thoughts and feelings are present for me in this moment?

_____

_____

_____

How can I set myself up to bring my best self to the world today?

_____

_____

What am I joyfully anticipating in the day(s) ahead?

_____

I'd like to create more _____ in my life by:

_____

Ways I intend to feel grounded today:

☐ Three deep breaths

☐ 60-second body scan

☐ Mindful check-in

Date: __ / __ / __   **Evening Reflections**

What is one thing today's experiences teach me about myself?

_____

_____

I'm ready to have this question answered:

_____

_____

Use this space to track how you practiced mindfulness throughout the day.

	When	Where
Morning		
Afternoon		
Evening		

Three things I am grateful for:

Morning Intentions

What thoughts and feelings are present for me in this moment?

_____

_____

_____

How can I set myself up to bring my best self to the world today?

_____

_____

What am I joyfully anticipating in the day(s) ahead?

_____

I'd like to create more _____ in my life by:

_____

Ways I intend to feel grounded today:

- ☐ Three deep breaths
- ☐ 60-second body scan
- ☐ Mindful check-in

Date: ___ / ___ / ___

Evening Reflections

What is one thing today's experiences teach me about myself?

_____

_____

I'm ready to have this question answered:

_____

_____

Use this space to track how you practiced mindfulness throughout the day.

	When	Where
Morning		
Afternoon		
Evening		

Three things I am grateful for:

Morning Intentions

What thoughts and feelings are present for me in this moment?

_____

_____

_____

How can I set myself up to bring my best self to the
world today?

_____

_____

What am I joyfully anticipating in the day(s) ahead?

_____

I'd like to create more _____ in my life by:

_____

Ways I intend to feel grounded today:

☐ Three deep breaths

☐ 60-second body scan

☐ Mindful check-in

Date: ___ / ___ / ___

What is one thing today's experiences teach me about myself?

_____

_____

I'm ready to have this question answered:

_____

_____

Use this space to track how you practiced mindfulness throughout the day.

	When	Where
Morning		
Afternoon		
Evening		

Three things I am grateful for:

Morning Intentions

Date: ___ / ___ / ___

What thoughts and feelings are present for me in this moment?

_____

_____

_____

How can I set myself up to bring my best self to the world today?

_____

_____

What am I joyfully anticipating in the day(s) ahead?

_____

I'd like to create more _____ in my life by:

_____

Ways I intend to feel grounded today:

☐ Three deep breaths

☐ 60-second body scan

☐ Mindful check-in

Date: ___ / ___ / ___

What is one thing today's experiences teach me about myself?

_____

_____

I'm ready to have this question answered:

_____

_____

Use this space to track how you practiced mindfulness throughout the day.

	When	Where
Morning		
Afternoon		
Evening		

Three things I am grateful for:

Date: ___ / ___ / ___

What thoughts and feelings are present for me in this moment?

_____

_____

_____

How can I set myself up to bring my best self to the world today?

_____

_____

What am I joyfully anticipating in the day(s) ahead?

_____

I'd like to create more _____ in my life by:

_____

Ways I intend to feel grounded today:

☐ Three deep breaths

☐ 60-second body scan

☐ Mindful check-in

Date: ___ / ___ / ___

What is one thing today's experiences teach me about myself?

_____

_____

I'm ready to have this question answered:

_____

_____

Use this space to track how you practiced mindfulness throughout the day.

	When	Where
Morning		
Afternoon		
Evening		

Three things I am grateful for:

Morning Intentions

What thoughts and feelings are present for me in this moment?

_____

_____

_____

How can I set myself up to bring my best self to the world today?

_____

_____

What am I joyfully anticipating in the day(s) ahead?

_____

I'd like to create more _____ in my life by:

_____

Ways I intend to feel grounded today:

☐ Three deep breaths

☐ 60-second body scan

☐ Mindful check-in

Date: ___ / ___ / ___

What is one thing today's experiences teach me about myself?

_____

_____

I'm ready to have this question answered:

_____

_____

Use this space to track how you practiced mindfulness throughout the day.

	When	Where
Morning		
Afternoon		
Evening		

Three things I am grateful for:

Morning Intentions

What thoughts and feelings are present for me in this moment?

_____

_____

_____

How can I set myself up to bring my best self to the world today?

_____

_____

What am I joyfully anticipating in the day(s) ahead?

_____

I'd like to create more _____ in my life by:

_____

Ways I intend to feel grounded today:

☐ Three deep breaths

☐ 60-second body scan

☐ Mindful check-in

Date: __ / __ / __

Evening Reflections

What is one thing today's experiences teach me about myself?

_____

_____

I'm ready to have this question answered:

_____

_____

Use this space to track how you practiced mindfulness throughout the day.

	When	Where
Morning		
Afternoon		
Evening		

Three things I am grateful for:

Morning Intentions

What thoughts and feelings are present for me in this moment?

How can I set myself up to bring my best self to the world today?

What am I joyfully anticipating in the day(s) ahead?

I'd like to create more _____ in my life by:

Ways I intend to feel grounded today:

☐ Three deep breaths

☐ 60-second body scan

☐ Mindful check-in

Date: ___ / ___ / ___   Evening Reflections

What is one thing today's experiences teach me about myself?

_____

_____

I'm ready to have this question answered:

_____

_____

Use this space to track how you practiced mindfulness throughout the day.

	When	Where
Morning		
Afternoon		
Evening		

Three things I am grateful for:

Morning Intentions

What thoughts and feelings are present for me in this moment?

_____

_____

_____

How can I set myself up to bring my best self to the world today?

_____

_____

What am I joyfully anticipating in the day(s) ahead?

_____

I'd like to create more _____ in my life by:

_____

Ways I intend to feel grounded today:

☐ Three deep breaths

☐ 60-second body scan

☐ Mindful check-in

Date: ___ / ___ / ___   Evening Reflections

What is one thing today's experiences teach me about myself?

_____

_____

I'm ready to have this question answered:

_____

_____

Use this space to track how you practiced mindfulness throughout the day.

	When	Where
Morning		
Afternoon		
Evening		

Three things I am grateful for:

Morning Intentions

What thoughts and feelings are present for me in this moment?

How can I set myself up to bring my best self to the world today?

What am I joyfully anticipating in the day(s) ahead?

I'd like to create more _____ in my life by:

Ways I intend to feel grounded today:

- ☐ Three deep breaths
- ☐ 60-second body scan
- ☐ Mindful check-in

Date: ___ / ___ / ___

Evening Reflections

What is one thing today's experiences teach me about myself?

_____

_____

I'm ready to have this question answered:

_____

_____

Use this space to track how you practiced mindfulness throughout the day.

	When	Where
Morning		
Afternoon		
Evening		

Three things I am grateful for:

Morning Intentions

What thoughts and feelings are present for me in this moment?

_____

_____

_____

How can I set myself up to bring my best self to the world today?

_____

_____

What am I joyfully anticipating in the day(s) ahead?

_____

I'd like to create more _____ in my life by:

_____

Ways I intend to feel grounded today:

☐ Three deep breaths

☐ 60-second body scan

☐ Mindful check-in

Date: ___ / ___ / ___

What is one thing today's experiences teach me about myself?

_____

_____

I'm ready to have this question answered:

_____

_____

Use this space to track how you practiced mindfulness throughout the day.

	When	Where
Morning		
Afternoon		
Evening		

Three things I am grateful for:

Morning Intentions

What thoughts and feelings are present for me in this moment?

_____

_____

_____

How can I set myself up to bring my best self to the world today?

_____

_____

What am I joyfully anticipating in the day(s) ahead?

_____

I'd like to create more _____ in my life by:

_____

Ways I intend to feel grounded today:

☐ Three deep breaths

☐ 60-second body scan

☐ Mindful check-in

Date: ___ / ___ / ___

Evening Reflections

What is one thing today's experiences teach me about myself?

_____

_____

I'm ready to have this question answered:

_____

_____

Use this space to track how you practiced mindfulness throughout the day.

	When	Where
Morning		
Afternoon		
Evening		

Three things I am grateful for:

Morning Intentions

What thoughts and feelings are present for me in this moment?

_____

_____

_____

How can I set myself up to bring my best self to the world today?

_____

_____

What am I joyfully anticipating in the day(s) ahead?

_____

I'd like to create more _____ in my life by:

_____

Ways I intend to feel grounded today:

☐ Three deep breaths

☐ 60-second body scan

☐ Mindful check-in

Date: ___ / ___ / ___

Evening Reflections

What is one thing today's experiences teach me about myself?

_____

_____

I'm ready to have this question answered:

_____

_____

Use this space to track how you practiced mindfulness throughout the day.

	When	Where
Morning		
Afternoon		
Evening		

Three things I am grateful for:

Morning Intentions

What thoughts and feelings are present for me in this moment?

_____

_____

_____

How can I set myself up to bring my best self to the world today?

_____

_____

What am I joyfully anticipating in the day(s) ahead?

_____

I'd like to create more _____ in my life by:

_____

Ways I intend to feel grounded today:

☐ Three deep breaths

☐ 60-second body scan

☐ Mindful check-in

Evening Reflections

What is one thing today's experiences teach me about myself?

_____

_____

I'm ready to have this question answered:

_____

_____

Use this space to track how you practiced mindfulness throughout the day.

	When	Where
Morning		
Afternoon		
Evening		

Three things I am grateful for:

Date: ___ / ___ / ___

What thoughts and feelings are present for me in this moment?

_____

_____

_____

How can I set myself up to bring my best self to the world today?

_____

_____

What am I joyfully anticipating in the day(s) ahead?

_____

I'd like to create more _____ in my life by:

_____

Ways I intend to feel grounded today:

☐ Three deep breaths

☐ 60-second body scan

☐ Mindful check-in

Evening Reflections

What is one thing today's experiences teach me about myself?

_____

_____

I'm ready to have this question answered:

_____

_____

Use this space to track how you practiced mindfulness throughout the day.

	When	Where
Morning		
Afternoon		
Evening		

Three things I am grateful for:

Morning Intentions

What thoughts and feelings are present for me in this moment?

_____

_____

_____

How can I set myself up to bring my best self to the world today?

_____

_____

What am I joyfully anticipating in the day(s) ahead?

_____

I'd like to create more _____ in my life by:

_____

Ways I intend to feel grounded today:

☐ Three deep breaths

☐ 60-second body scan

☐ Mindful check-in

Date: ___ / ___ / ___

Evening Reflections

What is one thing today's experiences teach me about myself?

_____

_____

I'm ready to have this question answered:

_____

_____

Use this space to track how you practiced mindfulness throughout the day.

	When	Where
Morning		
Afternoon		
Evening		

Three things I am grateful for:

Morning Intentions

What thoughts and feelings are present for me in this moment?

_____

_____

_____

How can I set myself up to bring my best self to the world today?

_____

_____

What am I joyfully anticipating in the day(s) ahead?

_____

I'd like to create more _____ in my life by:

_____

Ways I intend to feel grounded today:

☐ Three deep breaths

☐ 60-second body scan

☐ Mindful check-in

Date: ___ / ___ / ___

Evening Reflections

What is one thing today's experiences teach me about myself?

_____

_____

I'm ready to have this question answered:

_____

_____

Use this space to track how you practiced mindfulness throughout the day.

	When	Where
Morning		
Afternoon		
Evening		

Three things I am grateful for:

Morning Intentions

What thoughts and feelings are present for me in this moment?

_____

_____

_____

How can I set myself up to bring my best self to the world today?

_____

_____

What am I joyfully anticipating in the day(s) ahead?

_____

I'd like to create more _____ in my life by:

_____

Ways I intend to feel grounded today:

☐ Three deep breaths

☐ 60-second body scan

☐ Mindful check-in

Date: ___ / ___ / ___   # Evening Reflections

What is one thing today's experiences teach me about myself?

_____

_____

I'm ready to have this question answered:

_____

_____

Use this space to track how you practiced mindfulness throughout the day.

	When	Where
Morning		
Afternoon		
Evening		

Three things I am grateful for:

Morning Intentions

What thoughts and feelings are present for me in this moment?

_____

_____

_____

How can I set myself up to bring my best self to the world today?

_____

_____

What am I joyfully anticipating in the day(s) ahead?

_____

I'd like to create more _____ in my life by:

_____

Ways I intend to feel grounded today:

☐ Three deep breaths

☐ 60-second body scan

☐ Mindful check-in

Date: ___ / ___ / ___

What is one thing today's experiences teach me about myself?

_____

_____

I'm ready to have this question answered:

_____

_____

Use this space to track how you practiced mindfulness throughout the day.

	When	Where
Morning		
Afternoon		
Evening		

Three things I am grateful for:

Morning Intentions

What thoughts and feelings are present for me in this moment?

_____

_____

_____

How can I set myself up to bring my best self to the
world today?

_____

_____

What am I joyfully anticipating in the day(s) ahead?

_____

I'd like to create more _____ in my life by:

_____

Ways I intend to feel grounded today:

☐ Three deep breaths

☐ 60-second body scan

☐ Mindful check-in

Date: ___ / ___ / ___

Evening Reflections

What is one thing today's experiences teach me about myself?

_____

_____

I'm ready to have this question answered:

_____

_____

Use this space to track how you practiced mindfulness throughout the day.

	When	Where
Morning		
Afternoon		
Evening		

Three things I am grateful for:

Date: ___ / ___ / ___

What thoughts and feelings are present for me in this moment?

_____

_____

_____

How can I set myself up to bring my best self to the world today?

_____

_____

What am I joyfully anticipating in the day(s) ahead?

_____

I'd like to create more _____ in my life by:

_____

Ways I intend to feel grounded today:

☐ Three deep breaths

☐ 60-second body scan

☐ Mindful check-in

Date: ___ / ___ / ___

Evening Reflections

What is one thing today's experiences teach me about myself?

_____

_____

I'm ready to have this question answered:

_____

_____

Use this space to track how you practiced mindfulness throughout the day.

	When	Where
Morning		
Afternoon		
Evening		

Three things I am grateful for:

Morning Intentions

What thoughts and feelings are present for me in this moment?

_____

_____

_____

How can I set myself up to bring my best self to the world today?

_____

_____

What am I joyfully anticipating in the day(s) ahead?

_____

I'd like to create more _____ in my life by:

_____

Ways I intend to feel grounded today:

- ☐ Three deep breaths
- ☐ 60-second body scan
- ☐ Mindful check-in

Date: ___ / ___ / ___

Evening Reflections

What is one thing today's experiences teach me about myself?

_____

_____

I'm ready to have this question answered:

_____

_____

Use this space to track how you practiced mindfulness throughout the day.

	When	Where
Morning		
Afternoon		
Evening		

Three things I am grateful for:

Morning Intentions

What thoughts and feelings are present for me in this moment?

_____

_____

_____

How can I set myself up to bring my best self to the world today?

_____

_____

What am I joyfully anticipating in the day(s) ahead?

_____

I'd like to create more _____ in my life by:

_____

Ways I intend to feel grounded today:

☐ Three deep breaths

☐ 60-second body scan

☐ Mindful check-in

Date: ___ / ___ / ___

Evening Reflections

What is one thing today's experiences teach me about myself?

_____

_____

I'm ready to have this question answered:

_____

_____

Use this space to track how you practiced mindfulness throughout the day.

	When	Where
Morning		
Afternoon		
Evening		

Three things I am grateful for:

Morning Intentions

What thoughts and feelings are present for me in this moment?

How can I set myself up to bring my best self to the world today?

What am I joyfully anticipating in the day(s) ahead?

I'd like to create more _____ in my life by:

Ways I intend to feel grounded today:

☐ Three deep breaths

☐ 60-second body scan

☐ Mindful check-in

Date: ___ / ___ / ___

Evening Reflections

What is one thing today's experiences teach me about myself?

_____

_____

I'm ready to have this question answered:

_____

_____

Use this space to track how you practiced mindfulness throughout the day.

	When	Where
Morning		
Afternoon		
Evening		

Three things I am grateful for:

Morning Intentions

What thoughts and feelings are present for me in this moment?

_____

_____

_____

How can I set myself up to bring my best self to the world today?

_____

_____

What am I joyfully anticipating in the day(s) ahead?

_____

I'd like to create more _____ in my life by:

_____

Ways I intend to feel grounded today:

☐ Three deep breaths

☐ 60-second body scan

☐ Mindful check-in

Date: ___ / ___ / ___   **Evening Reflections**

What is one thing today's experiences teach me about myself?

_____

_____

I'm ready to have this question answered:

_____

_____

Use this space to track how you practiced mindfulness throughout the day.

	When	Where
Morning		
Afternoon		
Evening		

Three things I am grateful for:

Morning Intentions

What thoughts and feelings are present for me in this moment?

_____

_____

_____

How can I set myself up to bring my best self to the world today?

_____

_____

What am I joyfully anticipating in the day(s) ahead?

_____

I'd like to create more _____ in my life by:

_____

Ways I intend to feel grounded today:

☐ Three deep breaths

☐ 60-second body scan

☐ Mindful check-in

Date: ___ / ___ / ___

Evening Reflections

What is one thing today's experiences teach me about myself?

_____

_____

I'm ready to have this question answered:

_____

_____

Use this space to track how you practiced mindfulness throughout the day.

	When	Where
Morning		
Afternoon		
Evening		

Three things I am grateful for:

Morning Intentions

What thoughts and feelings are present for me in this moment?

_____

_____

_____

How can I set myself up to bring my best self to the world today?

_____

_____

What am I joyfully anticipating in the day(s) ahead?

_____

I'd like to create more _____ in my life by:

_____

Ways I intend to feel grounded today:

☐ Three deep breaths

☐ 60-second body scan

☐ Mindful check-in

Date: ___ / ___ / ___

What is one thing today's experiences teach me about myself?

_____

_____

I'm ready to have this question answered:

_____

_____

Use this space to track how you practiced mindfulness throughout the day.

	When	Where
Morning		
Afternoon		
Evening		

Three things I am grateful for:

Morning Intentions

What thoughts and feelings are present for me in this moment?

_____

_____

_____

How can I set myself up to bring my best self to the world today?

_____

_____

What am I joyfully anticipating in the day(s) ahead?

_____

I'd like to create more _____ in my life by:

_____

Ways I intend to feel grounded today:

- ☐ Three deep breaths
- ☐ 60-second body scan
- ☐ Mindful check-in

Date: ___ / ___ / ___

Evening Reflections

What is one thing today's experiences teach me about myself?

_____

_____

I'm ready to have this question answered:

_____

_____

Use this space to track how you practiced mindfulness throughout the day.

	When	Where
Morning		
Afternoon		
Evening		

Three things I am grateful for:

Morning Intentions

What thoughts and feelings are present for me in this moment?

_____

_____

_____

How can I set myself up to bring my best self to the world today?

_____

_____

What am I joyfully anticipating in the day(s) ahead?

_____

I'd like to create more _____ in my life by:

_____

Ways I intend to feel grounded today:

- ☐ Three deep breaths
- ☐ 60-second body scan
- ☐ Mindful check-in

Date: ___ / ___ / ___

What is one thing today's experiences teach me about myself?

_____

_____

I'm ready to have this question answered:

_____

_____

Use this space to track how you practiced mindfulness throughout the day.

	When	Where
Morning		
Afternoon		
Evening		

Three things I am grateful for:

About the Author

 **KRISTEN MANIERI** is a Certified Habits Coach, as well as a Certified Mindfulness Teacher through the International Mindfulness Teachers Association (IMTA). The author of *Better Daily Mindfulness Habits*, Kristen believes that when we actively engage in our growth and evolution, we can begin to live a more conscious, connected, and intentional life. Besides being a writer and coach, Kristen is the host of the *60 Mindful Minutes* podcast, which launched in 2017 and has produced inspiring and thought-provoking interviews with over 130 authors. Kristen holds a BA in English literature and communication studies. She shares her life with her two daughters, her husband, and their three cats. Connect with her at KristenManieri.com or on Instagram @kristenmanieri_.